A Place to Dance

How Richard Lamberty Brought Change to the Ballroom

Eric Rosswood *and* Richard Lamberty

Illustrated by Vincent Chen

Charlesbridge

To my husband, Mat. There's no one I'd rather dance through life with. And to our kids, Connor and Olivia, who always keep us on our toes.—E. R.

To Tom and Ava. Thank you for sharing my dream and making it come to life for so many. And to our dance community: April Follies belongs to you.—R. L.

To all my loved ones who taught my truest self to dance!—V. C.

Charlesbridge • 9 Galen Street Watertown, MA 02472
www.charlesbridge.com

Library of Congress Control Number 2024058939 (print)
Library of Congress Control Number 2024058940 (ebook)

ISBN 9781623546489 (hardcover)
ISBN 9781632892904 (ebook)

Printed in China • OPIC
The authorized representative in the EU for product safety and compliance is eucomply OÜ, Pärnu mnt 139b-14, 11317 Tallinn, Estonia, hello@eucompliancepartner.com, +33757690241
(hc) 10 9 8 7 6 5 4 3 2 1

Illustrations done in digital media
Text type set in Amasis MT
Designed by Diane M. Earley
Production supervised by Jennifer Most Delaney

Richard Lamberty wanted to be a dancer
for as long as he could remember.

When his first-grade teacher lined up the students by height, Richard was always right in front because he was the shortest. He would skip, spin, twirl, prance, and strut as he led everyone down the hall.

“Richard!” his teacher would call out. “Stop dancing and walk the right way!”

But for Richard, dancing was the right way.

It made him happy.

When he was ten years old, Richard taught himself how to clog. Clogging is a type of dance with loose, wild bodies and loud, stomping feet. Richard loved clogging so much, he did it everywhere: in class, in the school halls, even in the lunch line.

"That's not dancing," the other children teased. "That's just stomping!"

"There's more than one way to dance," Richard said as he clickity-clacked on by.

Dancing his own way brought him joy.

When he was a young teenager, Richard went to a ballroom-dancing camp. Instructors paired off the boys with girls. The partners waltzed, tangoed, and quickstepped. They did the rumba, the jive, and the cha-cha.

Richard liked partner dancing . . . but he was also jealous. The girls got to spin, twirl, and dip. He wanted to try those things, too.

"Boys can't do that," the teachers said. "Those are the rules."

Who made those rules? thought Richard.

He studied the girls in class and secretly practiced their moves on his own.

When Richard was sixteen years old, he took lessons at a new dance studio. The head instructor noticed Richard's enthusiasm and ability to mimic all the moves.

"I want you to teach here," she said.

"Me?" Richard asked in disbelief.

It turned out that learning how to dance everyone's roles had made Richard a better dancer, and a better teacher, too.

As the years passed, Richard taught at studios around the country, and his students won multiple competitions. Richard competed as well, but something was still missing. He wanted to dance both partners' steps while competing, but he couldn't find a place to do that.

Until one day . . .

He saw a poster in his neighborhood.

Richard couldn't believe it! He asked a few other instructors if they would dance with him at the Gay Games, but one by one, they all said no. The instructors were afraid they would lose their jobs if they competed as two men.

After lots of rejections, Richard finally found someone brave enough. His name was Tom, and the two of them agreed to be partners.

Dancing together made Richard and Tom happy.

To prepare for the games, they trained at night when the studio was empty, and after much practicing, they flew to Amsterdam to join the competition. Richard had never seen anything like this in his life.

Boys danced with boys.

Girls danced with girls.

People could dance any role they wanted, and sometimes they even switched roles in the middle of a dance!

Seeing everyone embrace different ways of dancing was encouraging. And hearing the audience cheer for it was thrilling.

When it was their turn, Richard and Tom moved freely across the floor.

They twirled around like a spinning top as they danced the Viennese waltz.

They glided like a paper airplane as they danced the foxtrot.

They raced and leaped like gazelles as they danced the quickstep.

And they swung back and forth like a pendulum as they danced the waltz.

Richard and Tom competed so well, they placed third in the world. When the games were over, they still wanted to dance with each other. So they did. But this time, they attended open practice dances in their neighborhood.

When they walked out onto the wooden dance floor together, they were met with angry stares and complaints. Some people even said they should leave. But others were . . .

Inspired!

More people grew curious about dancing in new ways. Many wanted to dance with their friends. Others wanted to dance with the person they loved. Everyone wanted to dance as joyfully as they possibly could.

But they couldn't find any competitions. The Gay Games only happened every four years, and other big competitions still had too many rules about how people should dance.

"That's not fair," Richard said. So Richard and his friends decided to create a new competition.

First they needed to find a place for the event: a large ballroom with a wooden dance floor and plenty of room for spectators.

Next they needed to find a DJ to play the music.

Then they needed to find people to judge the competition.

Finally they needed to invite the dancers.

The event was a success. Soon people from all over the world came to compete in what became known as April Follies.

Richard didn't have to worry anymore about breaking the rules. He had helped create a place with its own rules.

A place where people could dance with whomever they wanted.

A place where everyone belonged.

A place to dance . . . and be happy.

A Brief History

Richard Lamberty was born in Chicago, Illinois, on June 11, 1959. He had an early love for dance, and throughout his life, he studied various types of dancing, from clogging to country western. But nothing made him happier than ballroom dancing. He loved the challenge of performing difficult moves and the fun of working with a partner as a team. He also loved the flashy outfits.

But mainstream ballroom had strict traditions that everyone had to follow. Because of this, Richard was limited to dancing as a leader (the traditional male role) and never as a follower (the traditional female role). He was certainly never allowed to dance with another man.

Ballroom traditions prevented LGBTQ+ people from dancing the way they wanted. So some dancers created their own safe spaces where people could dance with a partner of the same gender in any role they wanted. In addition to the Gay Games, which were held around the world, some early same-gender dance events included the Stepping Out Studios competitions in the United States, the Pink Jukebox Trophy competition in the United Kingdom, the Australian Same-Sex Dancesport Championships in Australia, and the EuroGames held in various countries throughout Europe.

Not all same-gender couples wanted to dance in separate competitions. Some wanted to compete in mainstream competitions, too. But the National Dance Council of America (the organization that sets the standards for ballroom dance teachers and competitions) did not want that to happen. In 1999 they turned their traditions into formal rules, stating that only couples with a man leading and a woman following were allowed to compete.

In 2003, Richard Lamberty, Ava Kaye, and Tom Slater created the California Dancesport Championships for Same-Sex Couples. It was the first independent same-gender competition in the Bay Area. That event turned into April Follies, and people from all over the world came every year. April Follies became the largest and longest-running queer ballroom dance competition in North America.

At the time, same-gender ballroom dancing was growing in popularity in North America, but it was difficult for dancers to compete because different events had different rules. So, in 2007, Richard helped form the North American Same-Sex Partner Dance Association (NASSPDA) to create a set of standards for same-gender couples.

In 2019, after pressure from the mainstream dance community, the National Dance Council of America changed their rules to allow same-gender couples to compete. They also started allowing anyone to dance as a leader or a follower, regardless of their gender. Thanks to people like Richard, the world is changing, one dance step at a time.

Resources

Websites

Blackpool Dance Festival
https://www.blackpooldancefestival.com

European Equality Dance Association (EEDA)
https://equalitydance.eu

Federation of Gay Games
https://gaygames.org

National Dance Council of America
https://www.ndca.org

North American Equality Dancesport Association (NAEDA)
https://www.equalitydance.org

Anton Belov (left) and Richard Lamberty at the World OutGames IV in Miami, Florida, in June 2017.

Books

Allman, John Robert, illustrated by Luciano Lozano. *Boys Dance!* (American Ballet Theatre). New York: Doubleday Books for Young Readers, 2020.

Bouder, Ashley, illustrated by Julia Bereciartu. *Welcome to Ballet School: Written by a Professional Ballerina.* Beverly, MA: Frances Lincoln Children's Books, 2020.

Castrovilla, Selene, illustrated by Laura Freeman. *This Is Tap: Savion Glover Finds His Funk.* New York: Holiday House, 2023.

Flood, Nancy Bo, illustrated by Julianna Swaney. *I Will Dance.* New York: Atheneum Books for Young Readers, 2020.

Hernandez, Jess and Ruymán, illustrated by Teresa Martinez. *I Want to Dance in Pants.* Ann Arbor, MI: Sleeping Bear Press, 2025.

Sanders, Rob, illustrated by Steven Salerno. *Pride: The Story of Harvey Milk and the Rainbow Flag.* New York: Random House Books for Young Readers, 2018.

Stuart Nichols (top) and Richard Lamberty at the 5-Boro Dance Challenge in New York City on May 5, 2007.

A Note from Richard

When I first started competing in ballroom dancing, I followed the rules and did what was expected of me. I wore the same boring black costumes as all the other male competitors, danced to the same music, and led female followers across the floor. I easily fit in, but at the same time, I felt incomplete. I realized that I wanted to dance with another man and express myself freely.

I eventually met other ballroom dancers who were also gay, but they hid that part of their lives, afraid they would be judged if other people found out. They advised me to follow in their footsteps and hide my gayness as well, but I was never good at pretending to be something I was not.

When I discovered the world of gay cowboy dancing and same-gender ballroom dancing, it was transformational. Men with men; women with women; everyone flying around the floor. So free. So beautiful. I wanted to share my love of this dancing with all those who felt as limited as I had felt.

Together, Tom Slater, Ava Kaye, and I created April Follies: a safe space where everyone could love dancing and love who they danced with. It changed my life.

I learned that it can be easy to fit in with people who share your interests, but it's another thing entirely to feel like you truly belong. And sometimes, if you can't find a place where you feel like you belong, you have the power to create that space for yourself and others. There is always someone out there who has the same feelings as you do. You are never alone.

So, be yourself. Be proud. And keep on dancing!

Tom Slater (left) and Richard Lamberty, circa 2000.